Co-production:
Working together

A training course on this subject is available. Please contact Inclusive Choice Consultancy if you are interested.

geraldine@inclusivechoice.com

www.inclusivechoice.com

Edition 4.01 ©2019

ISBN 978-0-244-20715-1

Contents

Introduction 1

What is co-production? 3

How can we do co-production successfully? 9

What Co-production Isn't 11

Putting People First 13

How do we achieve inclusive co-production? 17

I know something you don't know – equality 29

Outcome Based Accountability 31

Challenging situations 34

Who is Helping Who? - Professional Boundaries 42

And Finally... 58

Appendix A: Co-production Checklists 60

Appendix B: 10 Top tips for effective co-production ... 65

Appendix C: Dos and don'ts of co-production 67

iii

Introduction

For the last sixteen years, I have worked as a parent carer in partnership with Manchester City Council to help my son Sam, who has various disabilities, become the confident young man he is today.

Sometimes it has been the most challenging of tasks, but most of the time I have shared Sam with outstanding schools and professionals. As a family, we have learned and grown stronger from the support we have received over the years, and I would like to think that those that provided the support have learned from Sam and us as a family.

Some of Sam's disabilities are rare or can be challenging, such as his Tourette's Syndrome. It was clear from the start that no single person could be the complete expert on what Sam needed, or what services should look like for him, and that includes Sam himself.

So, you might think, if no-one is the expert then how will Sam achieve anything? How will we know what

Co-production

is best for Sam without the expert telling us? Well the answers to these questions are: I am the expert; You are the expert; Sam is the expert. We all have expert knowledge in our professional and personal lives that if shared can make a positive difference to how service providers, service users and families can work together and share their knowledge.

As well as having positive experiences of working in partnership with services, I also have first-hand experience of what it feels like to be told how things will be done for Sam, where our voice, expertise and knowledge had very little meaning. This is so counter-productive when we are trying to promote less dependency on services and better community cohesion.

This book is about co-production but to put it simply, it's about the importance of working together, sharing knowledge and co-designing better ways to deliver services with service users, families, and our communities. That is co-production in a nutshell.

What is co-production?

Co-production challenges the traditional way of providing public services. It is a process that turns service users from passive recipients into active shapers of public services, because it means involving all stakeholders, including the people who use a service. Instead of simply asking users how satisfied they are with services, service providers instead engage front line staff, service users, the local community, and other relevant partners and ask *"What can we design and deliver together that will benefit our area?"*

There is not one definition of co-production that everyone agrees on because the approach is still developing and changing. For example, the Care Act defines co-production in the following way:

> *"Co-production is when you as an individual influence the support and services you receive, or when groups of people get together to*

Co-production

> *influence the way that services are designed, commissioned and delivered."*

Co-production is not just a word, it is not just a concept, it is a meeting of minds coming together to find shared solutions. In practice, co-production involves people who use services being consulted, included and working together from the start to the end of any project that affects them. When co-production works best, people who use services are valued by organisations as equal partners, can share power and have influence over decisions made.

Co-production acknowledges that people who use social care and health services have knowledge and experience that can be used to help make services better, not only for themselves, but for other people who need them also.

Real co-production means that people are truly involved in planning and designing services from the very beginning. Co-production is not something you do *to* people; rather it is something you do *with* people, from start to finish, at every step of the

What is co-production?

journey. Another way of describing co-production is "working together".

Definitions and language are important. Moving to a co-production paradigm needs to be more than just a change in words. There is a danger of assuming that the right words will be followed by the right actions. Real change is accompanied by a movement of resources to people who use services and to frontline staff.

There is no one sure-fire formula for co-production to work but there are some key features that are essential for co-production to become an everyday process in organisations:

- Defining people who use services as experts in their own right.
- Breaking down the barriers between people who use services and professionals.
- Building on people's existing capabilities.
- Including benefits where people get something back for having done something for others.

Co-production

- Working with peer and personal support networks alongside professional networks.

Here are some more definitions of co-production:

"A way of working whereby citizens and decision makers, or people who use services, family carers and service providers work together to create a decision or service which works for them all. The approach is value-driven and built on the principle that those who use a service are best placed to help design it."

"A relationship where professionals and citizens share power to plan and deliver support together, recognising that both have vital contributions to make in order to improve quality of life for people and communities."

The value of co-production

The values of co-production also link to the wider wellbeing agenda. Research commissioned by the New Economics Foundation suggest that there are five factors which contribute to our sense of wellbeing:

1. Connecting
2. Learning
3. Giving
4. Being aware
5. Being active

Co-production embodies these five factors by encouraging participation and mutuality, valuing the contributions of each participant and providing opportunities for learning. Confidence grows, new relationships are made, and a sense of community emerges, increasing the wellbeing of all participants and the resilience of the wider community.

There is so much to gain from embracing co-production. Your service will improve. Relationships between service providers and users can be much

Co-production

improved with this sense of co-ownership and equality. It's a fun and productive way of working together and you have the opportunity to see different perspectives that may differ from your own.

How can we do co-production successfully?

- Ensure appropriate and adequate resources are available to support co-production, for example, expenses, easy-read documents and access needs.
- Ensure frontline staff have everything they need for co-production, including time and flexibility.
- Ensure no one group or person is more important than another. Everyone can contribute given the right support.
- It's important to have good facilitation and listening skills, and to reflect and act upon what is heard. Acknowledge and respect what people who use services, their carers and families say.
- Ensure everything in the co-production process is accessible to everyone taking part.
- Before you start the work, decide together how you are going to work and what will make it successful, then stick to it.
- Accept that sharing power means taking risks. Take a chance! Learn to share power. Doing

Co-production

things differently means we can work across a whole range of issues that confront us.
- Work with the group to support a clear set of identified values with a collective sense of direction.
- Don't use jargon or acronyms, plain English is better for everybody.
- Create the expectation that people who use services, carers and families will be involved in every aspect of service planning, design and development and delivery at every level.

Refer to the appendices for more tips on successful co-production.

What Co-production Isn't

Co-production is not participation
Participation means being consulted while co-production means being equal partners and co-creators.

Co-production is not consultation
Co-production depends on a fundamental shift in the balance of power between public service professionals and users. The point is not to consult more or involve people more in decisions; it is to encourage them to use the human skills and experience they have, to help deliver public or voluntary services.

Co-production is not volunteering
Co-production is certainly about activity and giving time. But the traditional model of volunteering where there is a clearly defined role between providers and receivers does not promote equality or independence. Therefore, it is not the co-production model.

Co-production

Co-production is not about consultation or participation – except in the broadest sense where they do have their place. The point is not to consult more or involve people more in decisions; it is to encourage them to use the human skills and experience they have, to help deliver public or voluntary services.

Co-production should mean putting people first and working together as equal partners. Effective co-production informs and directs future decisions that are made at all levels of the process. It is recognising the skills, knowledge and contribution in this case, of service users and families and communities. Service users/families have living experience, so their opinions and experiences are crucial to the successful design, delivery, implementation, and monitoring of services changes.

Putting People First

Putting People First should always be at the heart of co-production. Putting people first shows an understanding that everyone has something to contribute and that exchanging these contributions is enriching for everyone concerned.

A good example of putting people first and working together is the work of Jean Vanier, who established the L'Arche Communities in learning disability services. Vanier did not see his role as caring for people with learning difficulties, but rather sharing his life with them and being open to receive and learn from them as much as to offer them support.

Jean Vanier once said,

> *"I am struck by how sharing our weakness and difficulties is more nourishing to others than sharing our qualities and successes".*

This is an important message for social care practitioners and agencies. We need to open our ears, our eyes and our hearts to the people we work with, which might involve sharing our vulnerabilities and concerns and allowing ourselves to be changed by genuinely 'meeting' with them in truly co-productive relationships. After all it is only what we would want for ourselves and our families and our communities.

Have you ever noticed when you ask someone to talk about a change they're making for the better in their personal lives, they are often really energetic? Whether it's training for a marathon, picking up an old hobby, or learning a new skill. For most people, self-transformation projects occupy a very positive emotional space. When it comes to self-transformation, you can't help but get a sense of the excitement. But there is another type of transformation or change that occupies a very different emotional space. The transformation of organisations and the way they work with their service users and other agencies.

First, let's acknowledge that change is hard. People naturally resist change, especially when it's imposed on them. People will resist change when they don't

Putting People First

understand why the change is happening and they don't feel part of the process of change.

Given the obstacles, what can we do to transform the way we work and interact with service users, families and communities so that change is empowering, energising and inspiring, rather than exhausting, frustrating and uninspiring? The answer to this is "Put People First".

Putting people first means giving people more choice and control over the help they get from your services, so they are able to help themselves more. To do that, we need to focus on five key imperatives, all of which have one thing in common, putting people first:

1. Inspire through purpose: connect your co-production project to something with a deeper sense of meaning and the organisation's larger purpose.
2. Go all in: go beyond short-term cost-cutting and start a new model of sharing information and co-production.

Co-production

3. Build capabilities: enable people with the skills and tools required to participate in co-production.
4. Instil a culture of constant learning: reinforce a shared goal and mutual learning.
5. Lead inclusively: Professionals need to be inclusive, engaging people right at the beginning.

Changes to the way we work, live and thrive in our communities will not happen overnight but using the Putting People First ethos will ensure that we stay on course for addressing:

- The disadvantage that individuals experience because of their gender, race, disability, age, sexual orientation, religion or belief
- Poverty and promoting greater independence and wellbeing in later life.
- Promoting better health and wellbeing for all.
- Building more cohesive, empowered and active communities.

How do we achieve inclusive co-production?

Well, the first thing we need is for everyone involved to commit to working in a co-productive paradigm and wherever you can use co-production, use it. Take time to think about where co-production could work within your service and how you're going to embed it, along with your everyday language?

To build trust between service providers, service users, their families and communities consider ways to hand over power from the "professional" to the service users.

Remember, there is no single formula for co-production but there are some key features that are present in co-production initiatives.

On the following page are some of the comments gathered from service users/carers about what works with co-production and what doesn't.

Co-production

What does and doesn't work with co-production?

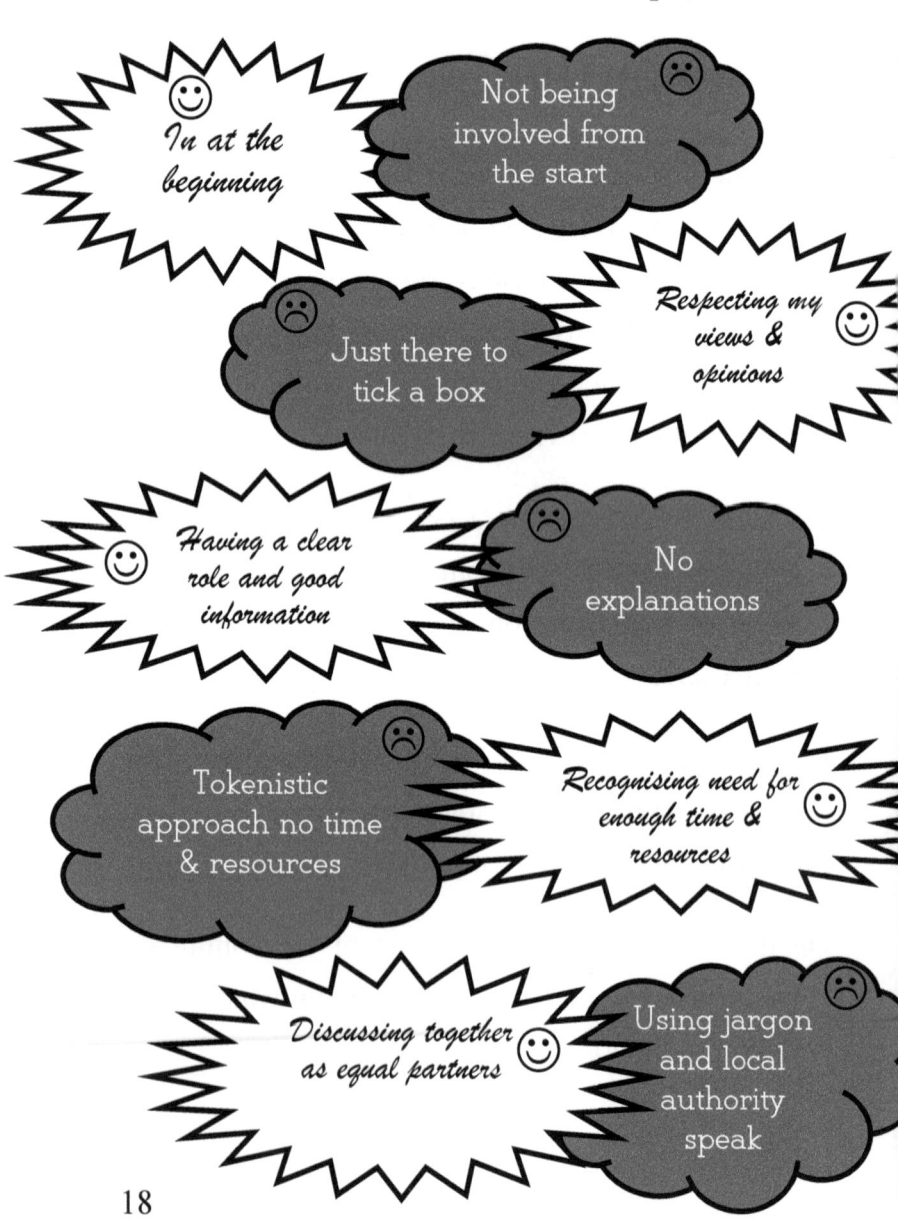

- 🙂 *In at the beginning*
- ☹️ Not being involved from the start
- ☹️ Just there to tick a box
- 🙂 *Respecting my views & opinions*
- 🙂 *Having a clear role and good information*
- ☹️ No explanations
- ☹️ Tokenistic approach no time & resources
- 🙂 *Recognising need for enough time & resources*
- 🙂 *Discussing together as equal partners*
- ☹️ Using jargon and local authority speak

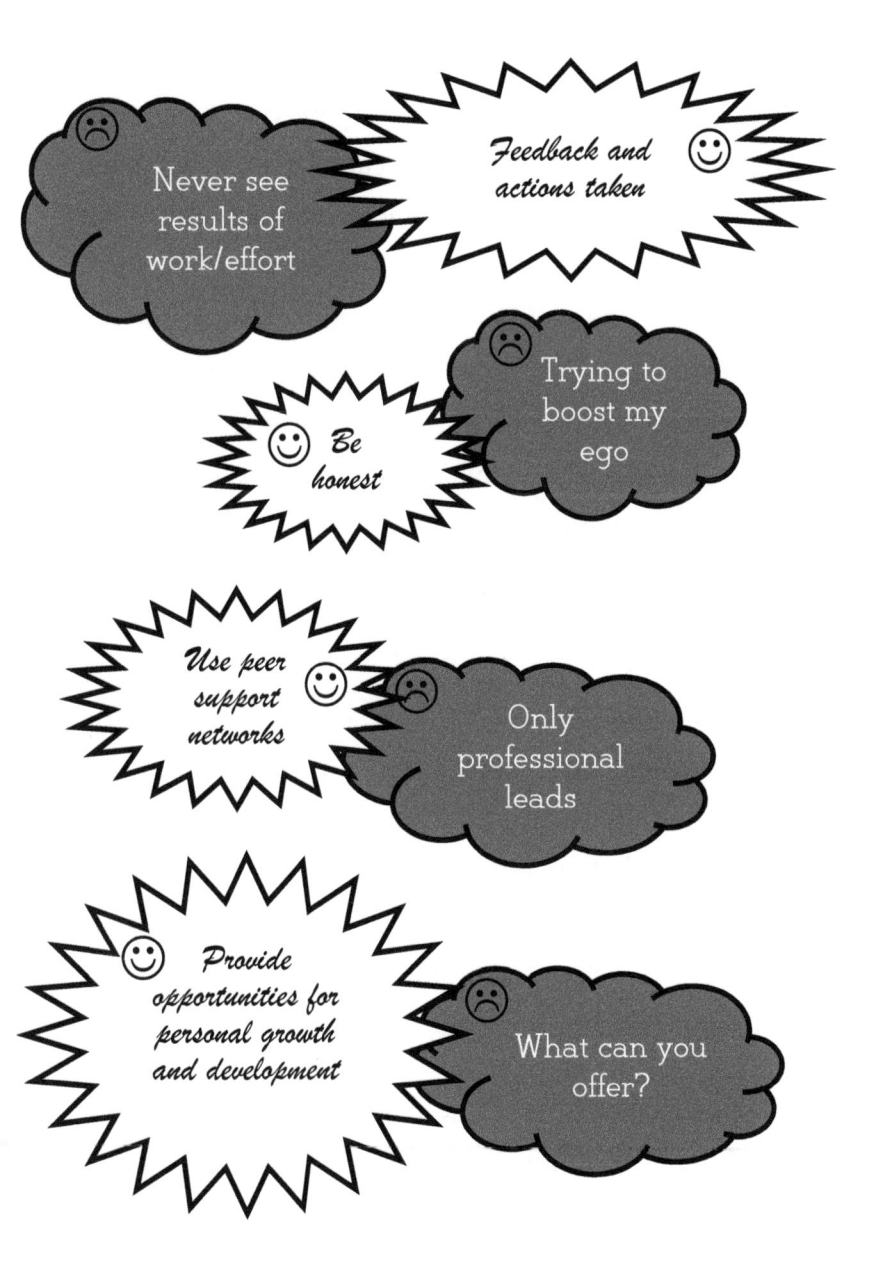

How do we achieve inclusive co-production?

- 😟 Never see results of work/effort
- 😊 Feedback and actions taken
- 😊 Be honest
- 😟 Trying to boost my ego
- 😊 Use peer support networks
- 😟 Only professional leads
- 😊 Provide opportunities for personal growth and development
- 😟 What can you offer?

Co-production

In at the beginning

In my voluntary role as a Parent Champion representative and as a parent carer of a young person with disabilities, I often come in contact with other parents/carers and young people, and one of the most common complaints about any co-production projects from them is not being involved at the very beginning of the process. It was often felt that decisions had already been made behind closed doors before they were involved. This does not promote a climate of trust and respect.

Being involved and included at all stages and levels of the process is key to building successful relationships and lasting and sustainable positive outcomes for all concerned. Recognising the expertise that parents/carers, young people and communities can bring to any co-production project is the first step to promoting equality within a working group.

The concept of "in at the being" also applies when working with other professionals. Let's say you are trying to get some members of your team to change the way they work because it's crucial to their job (which they know inside-out), but you didn't consult with them on this significant change. You never asked them about the impact this might have on their job. How do you think this would affect the dynamics, morale and job satisfaction within the team? How do you think it would affect you if you were only told halfway through the process of significant change to *your* job or even your personal life? I imagine you would be pretty brassed off to say the least.

Another example that comes to mind is one my friend told me about. She works for a Sure Start centre and one day she was told that everything was about to change. There was no consultation. She was crying when she told me her story as she felt that all her years of expertise counted for nothing, because she and the rest of the staff were not asked what they thought about the changes. She said:

> *"In our team we have expertise and valuable information about what worked well, what*

> *didn't, what's been tried before, what takes too long and what costs more".*

She was hurt and felt undervalued because she and her colleagues were not in at the beginning in any consultation and planning and didn't even know if they were going to keep their jobs.

Being in at the beginning gives a real sense of belonging, of being part of something and being included, and of course it gives a far more accurate picture of what needs to change.

Respecting my views and opinions
This is obviously self-explanatory. We should respect that every person has a right to an opinion. We should accept that not everyone will have an opinion that matches our own.

We should realise that opinions are not facts, are not objective and only reflect the individual's perspective. Showing that we respect other views can only strengthen any co-production plans, and invited

How do we achieve inclusive co-production?

participants will feel that they are not just there to tick a box, but to add real value.

Having a clear role and good information
People need to know their boundaries. They need to know what is expected of them. The need for role clarification is often identified as a significant issue and a barrier to good co-production. It is worth spending time thinking about what it is you want from your co-production partners when working together, otherwise this can cause confusion and resentment, so take time to plan for this.

The need for enough time & resources
If you don't factor in time constraints and resources when planning any co-production projects, then this could very well feel like a tokenistic approach to others. Time is something we are all short of but for service users their time is even more constrained because of their own work commitment, caring role and school timings.

Young people also have their own time constraints, for example their schoolwork or possibly their own caring roles. When it comes to co-production this needs to be considered and discussed with participants before any future plans are made.

It would be nice if resources were abundant whenever we wanted to work on a project, but this is rarely the case. There is nothing more disheartening and frustrating when you find out that your project is now being shelved because of lack of resources. When working on co-producing a piece of work keeping everyone in the loop as to what they can expect will go a long way to cementing respectful and lasting relationships.

Discussing together as equal partners
It is easy to think that equality is all about gender, pay or disability issues but there is another type of equality and that is the equality in working together. Using language or jargon can create big barriers to communication and successful co-production. It is an easy trap to fall into using jargon that you are familiar with, but this may not mean anything to others in your group.

How do we achieve inclusive co-production?

I am guilty of this when I talk to other parents of children with the same disabilities as my son. We just seem to fall into our own jargon and we just understand each other, but for someone who has no experience of this particular disability it can feel very alienating and elitist.

One of the biggest complaints people say when they come out of meetings or planning sessions was the use of jargon, which they found to be un-inclusive, alienating and sometimes intimidating.

Feedback and actions taken
Delivering regular constructive feedback is key to avoiding misunderstandings, and it also shows you have respect for other participants in your co-production project. Being made to feel isolated from the process of co-production is totally counter-productive. There is no point in telling participants that they are equal in the co-production process with their knowledge and experience being as valued as professional staff in the group, only to leave them out of key decisions or information.

A check-in on goal progress will need to be agreed so that performance expectations and outcomes can be monitored. The benefit of this approach is that you will improve your management and leadership skills as well as build on lasting partnerships.

Be honest
Even though there might be times when you can't divulge certain information to some members of your co-production group this does not mean that honesty cannot be maintained. As a parent carer, myself, who has contributed to a few co-production projects, I understand there are times when data protection might come into play. However, we cannot assume that this is understood, so a clear explanation of this will help with transparency and trust from the rest of the project members.

Provide opportunities for personal growth and development
When undertaking any co-production project, offering participants a range of incentives will help to embed the key elements of reciprocity and mutuality,

so that they are treated as assets to any co-production work, and not as an add-on or a tokenistic gesture.

In my role as volunteer Parent Champion representative for Manchester City Council I have been offered the chance to attend training courses where I can learn new skills to help in my Parent Champion role, as well as learning other skills that will help me in other areas of my life. Co-production is not about what the service users have to offer, but more about what they can gain from this process.

Use peer support networks
Instead of just using professionals as the best means of transferring knowledge and capabilities, practitioners could reach out to service users, carers, families, community lead organisations, charities and youth groups. Co-production that is only "professional lead" will fly in the face of what co-production is all about, which is, putting people first and working together. Promoting equality can only be achieved if the balance of transferring knowledge is treated with respect for others and not just professionals' opinion.

Co-production

Refer to the appendices for more tips on successful co-production.

I know something you don't know – equality

We all know something that other people don't know. I know something about bringing up a child with disabilities that you might not. I know stuff about Tourette's Syndrome that you might not, and I know how to cook a really good coffee cake! However, I don't know how your service works internally. I don't know about your professional time constraints, and I don't know your name.

So, we all know something others don't know and that is where co-production comes into its own. Co-production is about sharing knowledge. It's about prompting equality through an acknowledgement and respect for other people's expertise and experience.

There will always be those people that say, "how can working in partnership be equal when one part of that partnership is getting paid and it's their job?" My answer to this is that in co-production, we are passing

Co-production

and sharing knowledge and accepting that we all know something others don't.

We need each other to bring about lasting positive change to services in our communities and without each other's expertise this change cannot happen. The equality comes from respect, acknowledgement and inclusion.

Outcome Based Accountability

Outcome Based Accountability (OBA) is an approach that is recognised and used by the Department for Education. The OBA model offers tools and a coherent framework for strategic planning; evidence-based commissioning and monitoring what works to improve outcomes.

OBA is a disciplined way of thinking and taking action that can be used to improve the quality of life in communities and improve the performance of services and agencies.

OBA makes a careful distinction between outcomes and outputs. Outputs are defined as achievements, for example, recording extra attendance data for disabled people using services or alterations to the building. However, outcomes are achievements which lead to disabled people and families and communities being better off.

Co-production

This distinction is important because measuring success on the basis of outputs alone can be misleading. It is entirely possible for a service provider to deliver services that meet a wide range of outputs or process targets, including timeliness, staff recruitment and participation levels, yet still not succeed in improving outcomes for disabled people, their families and communities.

When we use OBA to improve our service to assess how well a programme, agency or service is working, we must ask ourselves:

- How much did we do?
- How well did we do it?
- Is anyone better off?

The question "Is anyone better off?" refers to the outcomes.

Have people benefited from the changes we have made? It is very important to measure how communities and people are better off. It is all very well spending time gathering data and changing policies, but if there is no measurable improvement in the life of the people that use your services, then it is all for nothing. Remember, you should be measuring outcomes, not just outputs.

Applying OBA to a co-production project is very important because co-production put you in direct contact with the very people that you are trying to improve services for. This means instead of just measuring your outputs you will ask yourself "how much did we do?" and "How well did we do it?", and most importantly ask your services users "Are you better off?"

For more information about OBA, get hold of the book "Trying Hard Is Not Good Enough" by Mark Friedman (ISBN 1439237867), the creator of OBA.

Co-production

Challenging situations

Before reacting to a challenging person or situation, consider what's driving them. Before you react, take a moment to imagine the world through their eyes. What pressures are they under at work, at home? What goals are they trying to achieve professionally or personally? What is happening right now that might be affecting the way they act? Once you've considered the options, settle on some possible explanations for their behaviour. You may or may not be right, but just the act of thinking about their world view will give you more stamina, more compassion and as a result you'll be more likely to find a way through.

Check your assumptions.
After our first few negative interactions with our challenging person or situation we've been 'primed' to think that all subsequent interactions will be negative. For example, what's your first thought when you see a peak-capped parking warden peering at your car windscreen? Is it "ahh, she's clearly

Challenging situations

admiring my pristine car interior!? Unlikely. It's the same with our challenging person. Once we're primed, we're likely to interpret what they do or say negatively. So, we respond negatively, and suddenly, we're in a vicious circle.

Look at this example below although it's a quite funny it also shows you the power of focusing on the negative and how that can have a detrimental effect on you and the people you interact with:

McGinty, a farmer, needed to plough his field before the dry spell set in, but his own plough had broken. "I know, I'll ask my neighbour, farmer Murphy, to borrow his plough. He's a good man; I'm sure he'll have done his ploughing by now and he'll be glad to lend me his machine."

So McGinty began to walk the three or four fields to Murphy's farm. After a field of walking, McGinty says to himself, "I hope that Murphy has finished all his own ploughing, or he'll not be able to lend me his machine..."

Co-production

Then after a few more minutes of worrying and walking, McGinty says to himself, "And what if Murphy's plough is old and on its last legs - he'll never be wanting to lend it to me will he?.." And after another field, McGinty says, "Murphy was never a very helpful fellow, I reckon maybe he won't be too keen to lend me his plough even if it's in perfect working order and he's finished all his own ploughing weeks ago...."

As McGinty arrives at Murphy's farm, McGinty is thinking, "That old Murphy can be a mean old fellow. I reckon even if he's got all his ploughing done, and his own machine is sitting there doing nothing, he'll not lend it to me just so watch me go to ruin..."

McGinty walks up Murphy's front path, knocks on the door, and Murphy answers. "Well good morning Mr McGinty, what can I do for you?" says Murphy.

Challenging situations

And McGinty says, with eyes bulging, "You can take your bloody plough, and you can stick it up your bloody arse!

Well poor farmer Murphy didn't know what hit him, but he was definitely the recipient of McGinty's negative thought process and assumptions.

It is interesting to note that although McGinty started out by thinking that farmer Murphy was a good man and that Murphy would be glad to lend him his machine, he ended up thinking and saying negative things about his neighbour. The story also shows that at the end McGinty really gains nothing.

If you approach any type of co-production projects with negative assumptions, chances are it will put you in a negative state of mind throughout the project and prevent you from developing long term positive relationship with others. And it the end you will have gained nothing but a headache!

Co-production

Four magic phrases

If someone is disrespectful or insulting to you (whether in a meeting or anywhere else) that's about them, so don't validate their behaviour with more disrespectful behaviour or comebacks. If you find yourself in a situation that could potentially be explosive, I want you to use one of the "four magic phrases" which go…

- "That's interesting, tell me more"
- "That's interesting, why would you say that?"
- "That's interesting, why would you do that?"
- "That's interesting, why would you ask that?"

Here are some examples of using these phrases:

- If somebody was rude enough to ask if you are gay you could start with "that's interesting, why would you ask me that"? Or "that's interesting why would you say that"?
- When a professional asks "Why are you saying that, I don't agree"? You say "that interesting, why would you say that"?

38

Challenging situations

- A group member refuses to work in a group or complete a task. You say "that's interesting why would you do that"?
- Your child's teacher says she has found a better way to support your child. You say "that's interesting, tell me more"

Try saying these four magic phrases out loud to yourself and practice doing this because it's an effective way to deal with challenging situations or people.

When somebody says something to you that you feel is disrespectful, rude or awkward often your ego rears its ugly head and you will often say something disrespectful back. In that moment, don't say the first thing that comes into your head, don't give in to that chemical reaction in your body where you can almost taste your anger. Instead remember your *Four Magic Phrases*.

Great communication comes from mutual respect. If you can't get that respect then make sure you are the one that remains cool, calm, collected and respectful.

Co-production

Then you will always be the one that stands out as the professional, whatever role you are in.

Your point of view

Yours is not the only truth. Each person has a different viewpoint. They will notice things that you have missed, and vice versa. Their view of "reality" is as valid to them as yours is to you. People who believe that everyone sees the world in the same way they do are setting themselves up for constant bewilderment. People who believe that others should see the world as they do are setting themselves up for constant disappointment!

People's actions make sense from their point of view, which we can never fully know or understand. Often their actions would seem crazy or wrong when judged in the context of our point of view – so when communicating with others, try to suspend your judgment.

When you want to persuade someone to change their mind, don't expect them to jump straight to your point of view. Why would anyone do that? Instead, start from a position that makes sense to them and is compatible with their values and beliefs, and build bridges to the place you want them to get to.

If you try to force someone to agree with you or give you what you want, chances are you will gain a reputation as being a bully with little regard for people's opinions and feelings. It is not always easy to leave behind a negative reputation, so it is worth spending time thinking about your personal style when it comes to interacting with others.

Who is Helping Who? - Professional Boundaries

Existing relationships and decision-making structures will need to adapt due to the nature and purpose of co-production, and organisations may feel that this compromises or de-stabilises professional boundaries. It is important to be very clear from the outset about roles and responsibilities, including things like expected time commitments, a code of conduct, and task descriptions for specific co-production roles.

The values and principles of co-production work well alongside the values and principles of Person-Centred Working - being open, honest, non-judgemental, valuing people's skills and contributions, and unlocking people's potential. With this approach it is possible to safeguard boundaries whilst working in a co-production way. It's all about being clear on expectations and roles.

For example,

> *Armad has recently completed a project with his local council. In this project, there were clear rules about co-trainer's roles and expected behaviours, and this proved very useful when there was some difficulty with a co-trainer on the first pilot session. Having a code of conduct helped to resolve this, the co-trainer was able to understand, reflect and continue to be involved.*

Co-designing services (managers and service users working together in the planning stages of projects) while important, must be accompanied by co-delivery (involving people in the actual service provision). However, it can also be useful to think about there being different levels of co-production.

For example:

- Where co-production already takes place in the delivery of services as people who use services and carers work together to achieve individual outcomes, but activities cannot

challenge the way services are delivered, and co-production is not really recognised.
- where there is more recognition and mutual respect, for example where people who use services are involved in the recruitment and training of professionals.
- where new relationships between staff and service users are created. Where people who use services are recognised as experts in their own right. There is respect for the assets that everyone brings to the process and an emphasis on all the outcomes that people value, rather than just those that the organisation values.

If our aim is to have successful co-production within our organisations and communities, then being flexible to new ways of working or taking different approaches to how we work will be a key to long term success. Having co-production wherever you can have co-production is the key to long term lasting respectful relationships between service providers, service users and their families.

Who is Helping Who? - Professional Boundaries

Do you believe me?

It is always mortifying not to be believed, and never more so than when we suspect that it is because we are supposed to be unworthy of belief. To believe someone is to validate their experience. To have your experiences, particularly negative experiences, validated by others is a normal part of being a human being. In my own tribunal case against a school, which I won, I was not believed by certain professionals when I tried to tell them what was happening to my son at his school. This hurt both me and my son, and for a time destroyed our faith in some of the services we were receiving.

Sometimes the people with whom you are co-producing will have their own stories of how they felt let down or mistreated by a service, and sometimes they will want to talk about this. It may have a direct correlation to the co-production group which might feel uncomfortable, but it is important that the person feels safe and believed to disclose their experience.

It is so important that you show respect when you are listening to someone who is telling their story. Even

Co-production

if you don't agree with them at the time, it may not be necessary for you to voice that opinion. As a parent carer, it is very important to me to be believed because I need to know that I have the respect and trust of any co-production team I am working in partnership with, otherwise equality, trust and respect just cannot exist within the group. Even if you do have doubts about a person's story, you must understand that this may be how they perceived the situation and it is very real for them.

Are you listening?
As a parent/carer and service user I can't tell you how much I value a service provider that genuinely listens to me, and I get told the same thing frequently by other parent/carers. It makes us feel that we are valued and that our viewpoint has merit.

It's the same when we feel we are not being judged for having an opinion that differs from the professionals.

Another part of any successful co-production work will be how you communicate as well as listen.

Communication is very important to every relationship, whether it be personal or professional. So when communication breaks down, it's important to understand why, solve it, and try to figure out how to prevent it from happening again in the future.

Whenever you have a miscommunication of any kind, it is probably due to at least one of:

- Believing there is only one reality (yours!).
- Responding defensively.
- Failing to listen.
- Choosing the wrong communication method.
- Failing to share information.
- Failing to be direct.
- Breaching confidentiality.

Part of having great communication skills is being willing to dissect your approach, behaviour and role when you find yourself involved in any miscommunication.

A trap easy to fall into is feeling angry and hurt if things don't go the way you wanted them to.

Co-production

Believing that your point of view is the only one worth listening to, or that what is true for you must be the same for everyone else will only lead to more miscommunication.

It never ceases to amaze me that when I see two politicians from different parties arguing over some policy or other, they both truly believe that their idea of what is best for the country is the only true point of view and therefore their policy is the only right way to proceed.

But then of course that changed in the UK with the coalition government in 2010, where two parties had to work in partnership with each other. Although this does not always run smoothly, I think it shows it is possible to work alongside others even though you may not always agree on what they think, do or say.

Trying to be flexible with other people's ideas will help lasting partnerships. Try to be honest with yourself when it comes to getting your message across. Refer to the list above, and keep asking yourself *"is there anything in that list that I did which got in the way of good communication and getting my message across?"* If the answer is yes then remember, it's never too late to change the way you choose to communicate with others.

Listen with your full attention
Have you ever been in a meeting where one minute you are listening to someone talking and the next you have drifted off to some other place in your mind? Or maybe someone is talking to you but you're only half listening because you are busy thinking about how you are going to respond. Sound familiar?

We process information faster than others speak so when we are supposed to be listening there is excess capacity in our brains to be doing something else. What most of us do is to:

- Listen
- React to what they've said
- Listen a bit more
- Plan our response
- Listen a bit more
- Find the right words and rehearse them

Co-production

- Listen a bit more
- SPEAK!

All these other activities prevent us from listening fully. Start by noticing when you've stopped listening and refocus yourself fully on what the other person is saying. Be confident that there is plenty of time to react, plan, rehearse and speak when it is your turn. Because if you're not listening you build very little rapport with others. Building rapport is important if you want your message to come across well and last in the mind of others.

Here are a few suggestions on how you can become a better listener:

- Listen with the intent of not responding. It does not mean you can't respond; it just means you're not planning it.
- Listening is not waiting for your turn to speak. Don't look like you're waiting to jump in, and that what the other person is saying is of no interest to you.

- We tend to hear what we are listening for. That's when a lot of breakdown in communications happens.
- We only hear what we understand. If we don't understand, or it makes no sense to us, we are not really listening or paying attention. So, if you don't understand, say so.

Self interest

As the parent of a young person with disabilities I have sat on many parent forums and other groups, and if I am honest one of the reasons I have attended these meeting is self-interest. I say self-interest but that's not the whole picture. Yes, I am there to find out what's new and could be of benefit to my own son, but I am also there to learn and pass on anything that might be of use to my friend, other families and my community. I pass on information about Manchester Local Offer to my GP's and schools.

There is nothing wrong with having self-interest when it comes to co-production, for professionals and service users. Self-interest is a great motivator and should be encouraged. However, it is how we conduct

Co-production

ourselves and how far we let our self-interest take over that is important to successful co-production.

I remember a group I was part of and there was this one participant that was causing problems within the group because their self-interest was the only thing driving them. They would constantly pick arguments and make accusations. The only time they were appeased was when they were talking about their personal story, which can of course have its place.

If you are faced with a situation like this, a code of conduct still applies. There should never be one rule for professionals and another for anyone else when it comes to co-production or true equality will never come into play. If it is made clear from the beginning of any co-production work that self-interest is natural but there is an expectation of the sharing and passing on of knowledge, things become much clearer.

Also, it's worth mentioning that every member is expected to adhere to any policy on code of conduct, but it is a safe place to have difference of opinions.

Engagement

Maslow's *Hierarchy of Needs* can help guide us when it comes to engagement with individuals and groups. Maslow's is a motivational theory in psychology comprising a five-tier model of human needs, often depicted as hierarchical levels within a pyramid.

Maslow argued that individuals needed to satisfy basic needs such as warmth, safety and security to then realise their own personal growth and development. The same theory can be applied to how an organisation treats and engages with service users, families and communities. Below you will see a diagram of the needs and how they can apply when you engage with service users:

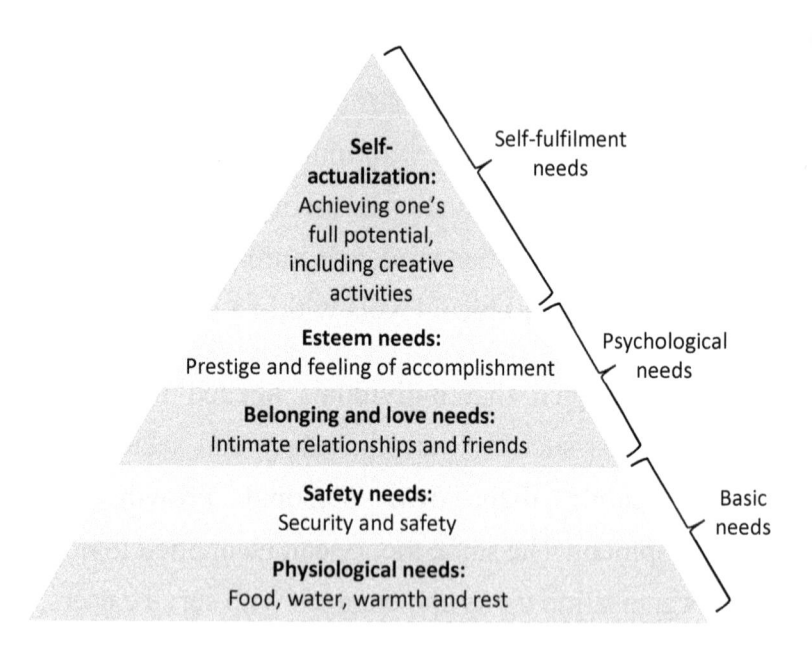

Co-production

Self-actualization: Achieving one's full potential, including creative activities — Self-fulfilment needs

Esteem needs: Prestige and feeling of accomplishment — Psychological needs

Belonging and love needs: Intimate relationships and friends

Safety needs: Security and safety — Basic needs

Physiological needs: Food, water, warmth and rest

Physiological needs: To survive, people need air, food, water, sleep, and so on. How does this relate to service users? They need to feel comfortable in the environment that you are providing for any work that you are doing together.

If working conditions are uncomfortable, such as too hot, cold or noisy, they probably won't advance to the next level in the pyramid — they simply won't have the motivation to engage. Similarly, access to such things as breaks, food, drinks, and so on. All this will need to be factored in for successful engagement to happen.

Location is an important factor. Arranging meetings or workgroups at a venue and time that is best for you will not always be suitable to other participants and could be another barrier to engagement.

Questions you might want to ask participants when planning any co-production work are:

- Is the venue accessible and within reasonable traveling distance for participants?
- Do you have funding for travel expenses?
- Are start and end times realistic or a barrier?

Safety: People must feel that they, their family, their property, and other resources are safe. When it comes to service user engagement, if they have to worry about their personal safety - for example, being threatened because of their personal views or their views being held against them - morale will suffer and engagement will likely cease. For any co-production to become successful, participants have to feel safe to have their own views and to feel valued.

Love/belonging: Not surprisingly, creating a sense of belonging is a key aspect of building an engaged culture. When we feel part of something, when we understand why we are doing what we are doing and when we emotionally connect and understand the bigger picture of why we are involved in a project then motivation will follow.

Esteem: Esteem is a person's belief that she is doing a good job and that her contributions are recognised. People want to feel that they're achieving and that their contributions matter and are recognised. Confidence is key. If a person has confidence, that person will shine. The same principle holds true with engagement. If the person believes in themselves and believes (thanks to recognition) that others believe in them they'll be more engaged and productive.

Self-actualisation: A key aspect of self-actualisation is ensuring that when working on any co-production,

Who is Helping Who? - Professional Boundaries

participants are only put in positions for which they are capable. Of course, people should feel challenged, but you don't want them to be in over their heads, because ultimately, this will erode engagement.

Don't treat service user's the way you want to be treated. This might sound like the opposite of normal advice, but it would be a mistake to assume that everybody wants to be treated like you do! Why? Because the very things that build satisfaction and trust in one culture can be the very things that destroy it in another.

We are culturally diverse in our communities so just being aware that someone's reaction could be different from yours will help you be better prepared when undertaking co-production work.

And Finally...

Co-production is not something that happens overnight. It takes time to build up relationships and trust within groups or individuals. In fact, in my experience when co-production is forced or rushed it can have a negative effect on existing relationships between service providers, service users, families and communities.

Take time to think about where co-production could work within your service, and how you're going to embed co-production in your service. The more you use the term co-production in your everyday language the more it will seem like second nature to do it.

I remember (many years ago, now!) when I first heard the terms "Person Centred" and "One Page Profiles" I thought it was just more trendy buzz words but much further down the line I can't imagine services not working with my son in a person centred way, or Sam not having a one page profile to help others understand what's important to him.

And Finally...

I know sometimes it is easy to dismiss new terminology or ways of working as just another fad but if we would have done that with the concept of person-centred approaches, I think we would be a lot worse off as service providers now.

So, take time to think about who are your partners, who else is working in a co-production paradigm. What do these other organisations, charities, communities, parent/carers, and young people groups know that you could learn from?

Remember there is a wealth of knowledge and skills between you, service users, families, young people and our communities and the way to tap in to that is by sharing what we all know and co-producing better services and ways of working.

Appendix A: Co-production Checklists

This check list identifies key questions you will need to consider in developing your Engagement Plan. Working through these questions in the planning stage of any co-production work you undertake will better prepare you.

Check list 1

What is the title of your co-production?
Title:
Purpose:
Who needs to be involved?
Are there any statuary obligations?

Appendix A: Co-production Checklists

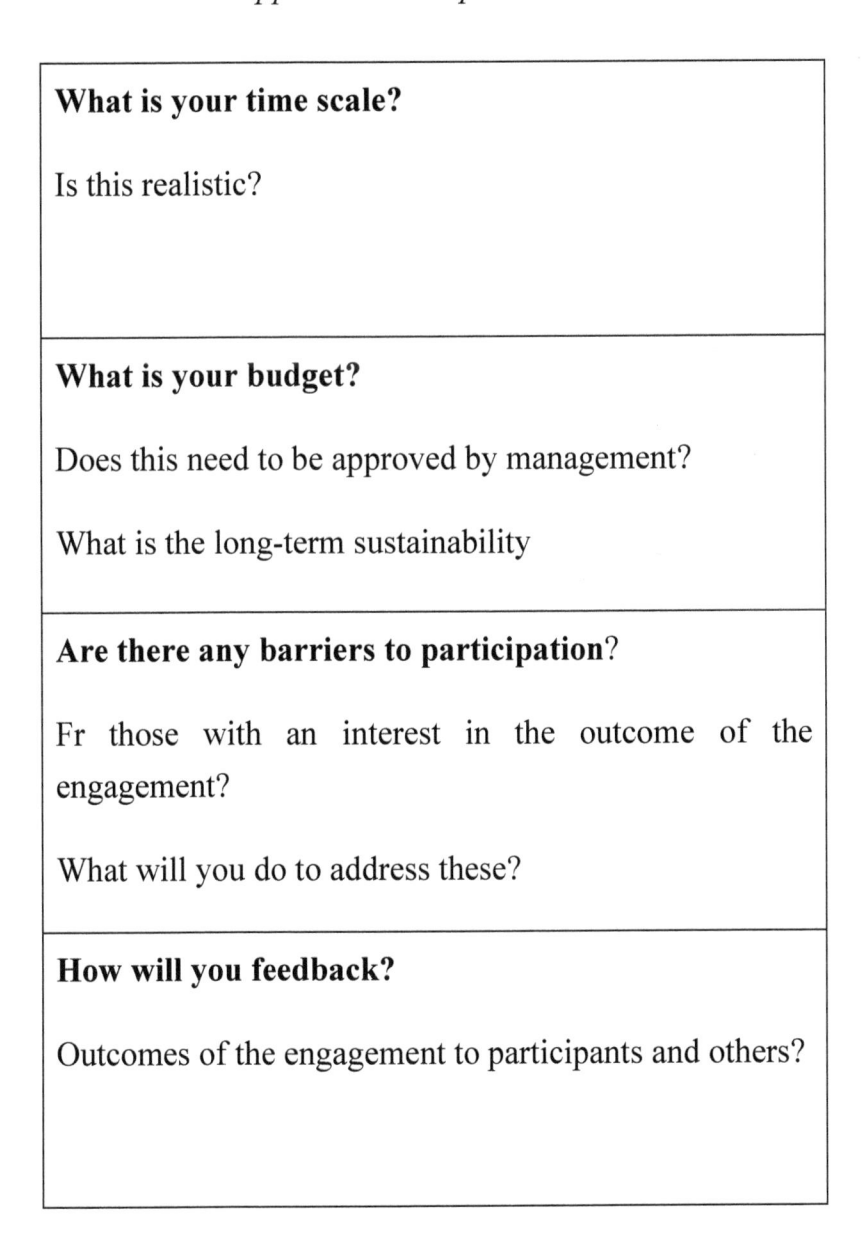

What is your time scale?   Is this realistic?
What is your budget?   Does this need to be approved by management?   What is the long-term sustainability
Are there any barriers to participation?   Fr those with an interest in the outcome of the engagement?   What will you do to address these?
How will you feedback?   Outcomes of the engagement to participants and others?

Co-production

How will you measure?

Whether the engagement has been successful?

Check list 2

Some things you may wish to consider at this stage:

- Have you considered the involvement of all groups with an interest in the decision? How will people outside the group contribute to the decision?
- Are the intentions and responsibilities associated with co-production clear to everyone involved?
- Are the methods you are using the most appropriate? Are there opportunities to be more creative?
- Does everyone involved have the skills and capabilities to participate in a meaningful way? If not, does your engagement plan allow time and resources for training and capacity building?
- Does everyone involved have access to the same information?

Co-production

- How will you deal with conflict or differing expectations? How will decisions be made if consensus cannot be reached?
- How will you monitor that you are doing what you planned?
- How will you deal with unexpected developments? Are there options for flexibility?

Appendix B: 10 Top tips for effective co-production

1. Co-production must start as an idea that blossoms with everybody involved having an equal voice.

2. Come to the table with a blank agenda and build it with people who use your service, their carers and families.

3. Involve people who use services, carers and their families in all aspects of a service – the planning, development and delivery.

4. In order to achieve meaningful, positive outcomes, everybody involved must have the same vision, from front line staff to management/board members.

5. Start small and build up to bigger projects, letting service users lead, not professionals.

Co-production

6. Acknowledge that a range of skills are needed for co-production.

7. Recruit the right people that support co-production.

8. People who use services, carers and families should be clear about what their expectations are and be fully engaged in the process.

9. People who use services and their carers know what works, so you can't get it right without them.

10. Don't take responsibility for solving every problem - allow the group to find collective solutions.

Appendix C: Dos and don'ts of co-production

Do co-production if...

- You detect 'outrage' among some of your community, if people are banging the table about a service.
- There's doubt about the design of service you want.
- You need the active participation or acceptance of your service users.
- You're happy for your participants to take over your project entirely.
- You need a solution on the same scale as the problem, i.e. how else are you going to deal with obesity?
- You can be honest with people about your priorities and resources.
- You're prepared for ideas to come from anywhere and anybody.
- You're happy to go where your patients take you.

Co-production

- You have the time and resources to maintain participants' energy during the dark weeks of the project.

Don't do co-production if...

- You think you know precisely the service that you require.
- You aren't prepared to fail.
- You can't leave your agenda (or strategy) at the door.
- You can't regard your critics as your prime resource.
- You can't regard peoples' outrage as important as your evidence, statistics and strategy.
- You haven't got access to all levels and all stakeholders.
- You aren't prepared for this to take far longer than you imagine.
- You can't afford to take lots of small steps to get where you want to go.
- You think you might not be able to spot or value people's capabilities, time or energy.

Appendix C: Dos and don'ts of co-production

- You haven't got someone facilitating the project that has good connections both above and below in the health organisation.
- You haven't got the funders behind you
- You think co-production is a way to save money on services.
- You're not prepared to follow through with something meaningful to your participants.
- You feel that getting close to people, or rewarding them for their time and energy, may violate your ethics.

Co-production

Useful websites for co-production

Visit the Inclusive Choice Consultancy website which has a page dedicated to co-production:

- www.inclusivechoice.com

Other useful sites:

- www.scie.org.uk/publications/guides/guide51/what-is-coproduction/
- www.virtualstaffcollege.co.uk/wp-content/uploads/co_production.pdf
- www.virtualstaffcollege.co.uk/wp-content/uploads/changing-professional-behaviour.pdf
- www.coproductionscotland.org.uk/about/what-is-co-production/
- www.seemescotland.org/media/7287/co-production-self-assessment-framework.pdf